WE THE SISSY PEOPLE

Explaining the character, moral and societal decline of the United States

GEORGE JEFFERSON ADAMS

DEDICATION

To all Americans who have made it their business to make
the world a better place, while acknowledging that the
United States has its faults, weaknesses and who recognize
that there are other great nations on earth.
And to the Other Americans who are oblivious of the
diminishing greatness of their country.

Introduction

Of nations and greatness

The United States of America considers itself and is often considered the "most powerful nation" on earth. This myth has been fed everyone who cares to listen, everyone who doesn't care to listen, Americans and foreigners alike, and frequently, no one questions its validity. Americans especially are appreciative and largely unquestioning of this tale, this theme, this idea of greatness. Where the greatness of the nation is in question or discussed, it is almost taken for granted – and accepted without question - that it is the greatest nation on earth.

The greatness of the nation and perhaps the frequent psychological reminder and expression of this belief is reinforced at every occasion, during practically every event worth its salt. It is expressed in the renditions of the national anthem (admittedly, done at most events even in foreign countries), at little league meetings, town halls, convocations, on account of no occasions at all, citizenship ceremonies, and a myriad of events.

It is expressed in its jet fighters and bombers flying over a baseball stadium, to the playing of a World Series between the New York Yankees and the St. Louis Cardinals (world? series?) It leads to an unmistakable belief, a demonstration at every occasion, that the United States is the greatest nation on earth.

Newsflash: every nation is the greatest nation on earth – including North Korea, Monaco and Tuvalu – but that is a topic for a different time. The greatness of each nation notwithstanding, it is amazing how much the greatest nation on earth is "ungreat."

An examination of several aspects of the United States of America paints a completely different picture from that of greatness. Very credible arguments can be made about how the United States of America has been, over time, militarily incompetent, economically on the brink of disaster, its citizens morally, socially and emotionally weak, the political system rigged, ineffective and incapable of making significant and important changes when needed. The arguments show that the United States projects one picture to the outside world, but internally, it is weak and corrupt.

In addition, despite all the perceptions of how terrible other political systems are, the United States' political system is extremely corrupt and wanting. The primal fear and notion of "protection" that characterizes the daily life of an American has given the government overwhelming control, and has left its citizens cowed by the very government that was established "by the people, for the people".

The United States, to the undiscerning eye, appears near perfect: all those Wall Street types, dressed in suits with their mochas, rushing here and there to run the affairs of the world. This image does not show those homeless, destitute, and otherwise ill, who are well hidden from the general public, in projects, group homes and other places the ordinary person has no reason to visit. There is significant social isolation and active "warehousing" of these "undesirables" who include its prisoners, old people, the poor, blacks, and the mentally ill, disabled, fat and other otherwise economically unproductive members of its society.

A critical study of the United States' society shows a people that are economically unproductive, whose forward progress lurches from one lucky break to the next. It reminds one of Otto von Bismarck's near-lament, that

"God has a special providence for drunks, fools and the United States of America."

The study shows a people who, despite this special providence, are resigned to spending their life in unhappiness, in pursuit of the dollar, believing that it will give them happiness. As such, they work fifty hours a week, fifty weeks a year, slaving away to generate wealth for its richest and believing that money, rather than personal relationships, will change their lot.

The geographical disconnect between Americans and the rest of the world is especially one to marvel. Even as the country has presumably assumed the leadership of the world, either due to isolation, general disinterest or the fact that most news networks devote ten seconds to foreign news – unless it is a characteristically terrible occurrence – the larger population of the United States of America is painfully ignorant of world geography, believing that theirs is the centre of the universe and forgivably so.

This treatise reviews the different facets of the American nation, generally examining the myths of its greatness from an external, perhaps biased perspective. But who is to say that a counter-biased perspective is not deserved is not necessary, or even desirable? After all, it is all that the good citizens of the United States have received through different sources - politicians, parents, and media - and without a counter-balance; the pride can get to the point of delusion.

And then, in the absence of countervailing perspectives, a nation begins to slide into irrelevancy, fed by its illusions of grandeur and greatness. This can make the United States of America oblivious to the changes that are happening elsewhere in the world, including the rapid rise of other countries. It will sound extremely critical, but it should be taken in good faith, as an opportunity to see how others see the United States of America.

A violent beginning

The United States of America has its beginnings in rather unusual circumstances: a band of rebels, fleeing an arguably atrocious and self-important King, invading a territory occupied by a people perhaps not considered worthy of occupying the land. Over time, the pursuit of safety and a new home away from home became an economic pursuit, one that would be expressed in such ideas as manifest destiny.

Unlike the United States, most countries have generally come into being through unification of their several tribes, kingdoms and other constituent groups. Arguably, there were invasions, occupations and whole displacement of populations – who can forget South Africa's Boers, or Rhodesia's white farmers deciding that Rhodesia / Zimbabwe was going to become a "whites-only" territory away from Britain? Australia does not have a better reputation: its current majority started as a prison colony, and worked itself into a respectable – at least somewhat – country. One wonders whether there is a collective wish that Darwin had not come up with that evolutionary theory that has since been widely discredited.

This in no way argues that nations are not expected to be founded based on the conditions under which most have thrived: bloody, predatory and through general displacement, murder and relocation of native populations. On the other hand, this has been the case in history; the difference is the level of acknowledgment of the history of such nations. Great nations generally do not acknowledge these failures; they are part of nation building and each nation probably has them.

Other "great" nations have had their share of atrocities against other populations: in this respect, the United States finds itself with many friends. The Germans tried – unsuccessfully – to exterminate the Herero, as recently as a century ago, and blithely carted away skulls to display in museums in Germany. These stood as rather ignorant evidence of the German racial superiority until in the third millennium, it was not "proper" to continue holding these skulls.

The United States of America bears greater scrutiny, mostly because it has developed amnesia about its development in history. Only sixty or so years ago, a significant part of its population, after being slaves for hundreds of years, were still sitting at the rear of the bus, second class citizens, even after building the country. How does such a country then move forward and become the moral voice of society? Is its memory so short? Compared to countries that have existed for five thousand years – it is quite amazing how it takes the moral high ground.

The violent beginnings not only saw the near total decimation of the American Indian peoples; those that were not shot, lynched and dispossessed of their trove and treasure were driven into enclosures, aptly named *reservations*. Here, dispossessed, ridiculed as backward and hidden from the rest of America and the world, they were fed whisky and dried beef and allowed to run their own societies with a semblance of their former dignity, forgotten, warehoused and kept from view as the United States went about the business of preaching democracy, equality, better treatment of minorities, human rights, economic development and all other largely unworkable *beliefs and approaches*.

The beginnings of the United States have some effect on its current character and people. It is very unlikely that you can play a national anthem whose words in part contain words such as "bombs bursting in the air" over and over again, and not expect it to have some effect on *we the people*. True, there are many national anthems that bespeak of evil, violence and war – there are also many countries with gentle national anthems that bespeak of prayer, hope, togetherness and other peaceful aspirations and designs for self and neighbour.

These presumably are subsumed and relegated into the history of irrelevance by the fact that those countries are neither world leaders, nor present themselves as some country designated to lead the world. In this respect, the United States of America opens itself up to harsher scrutiny of its people, systems and overall society.

Back to nations' greatness: if one were, for a moment, to pose and question the narrative of this being the "greatest nation on earth", one might wonder about the criteria for such determination. Is it the military? The military makes a country only as great as the weakness of other countries that one fights. And if one recalls recent history, the United States won the battles but lost the wars in Iraq and Afghanistan. And basically declined to fight the most important fight: against the Soviet Union. But we shall talk more about this later.

There is one place in which the United States leads a lot of other countries, even countries in its league. For instance, it has the highest percentage of prisoners in the world, and especially among developed countries. It also has the highest prevalence of individuals diagnosed with mental health illnesses and the highest number of gun deaths each year. Rather depressing statistics.

Perhaps greatness is in its infrastructure? Ok, Dubai has some rather impressive infrastructure [ok, they have one super-tower and a few man-made islands] and mostly camel tracks, some caves and tents. Is it transportation infrastructure, such as roads? China, Japan and most of Western Europe has better road infrastructure, networks of high speed trains, tunnels under the water and through mountains.

Is it per capita GDP? It is also true that while this tops $50,000, the total national debt is rather high, so in effect we are dividing other peoples' money by the population, never mind that close to 30 percent of the United States population lives under federal poverty guidelines *and* Monaco and Liechtenstein have a higher per capita GDP (ok, maybe they don't count, they are not real countries). Kuwait and Qatar have comparable per capita GDP.

One might consider other variables, but even in education, the United States has fallen to sixteenth among the major industrial nations. Also, it may be the case that the per capita GDP is high, but what does majority of the population use it on? Buying medication and seeing therapists: certainly, the Nordic countries – even with higher tax rates – are generally happier, if the Planet Happiness Index is to be believed.

That leaves the military. True, the United States spends more than the next fourteen countries combined on her defense, but – and this will be in the first section of the booklet – in the only major war that she could have fought as a superpower, the United States *blinked* and opted to wait out the Soviet Union. In the wars it has fought during its *reign*, the victory rate is dismal, unless you count winning against Grenada and Panama, which even Western Sahara could probably win a war against.

Consider this: the United States did not win in the Korean War (who fights a war for sixty years?), actively lost the Vietnam War, withdrew the marines from Beirut (lost against Lebanon?), needed the help of thirty some countries to fight Iraq in the first Gulf War and about the same number to fight in the second Gulf War, eventually "lost" that particular war and sort of lost in Afghanistan after 2001. And remember, the greatest attack against the United States during peacetime and its supremacy was leveled against the country using box-cutters and knives on an airliner. *When did the United States ever win a war?*

Every nation believes itself to be great. There is no doubt that while immigration and the desire to go visit, sometimes relocate to a different country, including significant immigration to the United States, often gives ammunition to the perception that the United States is *greater* than all those other countries. It is one thing to believe that you are the greatest nation on earth; the issue arises when the greatest nation tries to remake every nation in its own image.

This has lessons for practically every great nation on earth – or purporting or aspiring to be. It is amazing that nations, great and small, do not learn the clearly obvious lessons of history. In modern times, there has been no record of a foreign nation invading and winning a "nationalist" war. It is simple: national sentiment is strong, everywhere, and really, after an invasion there is nothing to lose except the very territory folks fight for.

The important takeaway here is that the Kingdom of Brunei Darussalam, as much as Tuvalu, Monaco, Tonga, Lesotho and Swaziland (both completely surrounded by South Africa) and even Mongolia – are all full of citizens who are patriotic and very passionate about their countries and absolutely, unshakably convinced that their country, bar all others, is the greatest on earth, even if its greatest export is a King who prides in having a new wife each year or its greatest export is – sand.

So what is wrong with the United States? This tratise seeks to review some areas where the United States of America may use alternative perspectives on its role, greatness and aspects of its relations with others – including a candid view of what others have thought about the United States.

History

South Sudan, Kosovo and Montenegro are some of the newest countries in the international sense: that is, recognition as sovereign states, a coveted, often well-earned status that is often conferred by the General Assembly of the United States. Each of these countries is, in the context of other countries' existence, relatively infant: South Sudan is less than three years into its existence.

The United States has existed, in the greater scheme of things, for a significantly shorter period than other major countries. A history of less than two hundred and fifty years pales in comparison to the histories of countries like the United Kingdom, which put out the Magna Carta in 1225AD, or Syria, whose capital Damascus dates back about 5,000 years, or China, which has a similarly long existence.

The United States of America, as discussed earlier, came into being in the current form much more recently, and as such, can be seen as a young teenager as these things go. It is always amusing to see the attempt at imposition of statehood – be it democracy or some other form of government – based on a two hundred year history, much of which majority of its citizenry – common people (before Jackson), women (before the suffrage movement) and blacks (before the civil rights era) were excluded from the participation in activities relating to citizenship.

Numbers, winning

If there is one thing that obsesses the United States, it is the concept of numbers. America and its people are obsessed with numbers, be it birthdays, being on time, baseball ERAs, football touchdowns, dollars, jump-shots, percentages of people disapproving of the government, numbers drive everything. And it is not just small numbers: for instance, in comparison with football (you know, the one that is actually played with feet, which Americans call soccer), American football goes for big numbers: each touchdown is worth a whooping six points. It is not clear why this is the case – after all, hockey and baseball use the single point for each score.

It is surprising to many Americans then, that numbers are often not that important. It aggravates them that most foreigners – especially in still-traditional communities – cannot even keep good time; you see, the concept of numbers is fairly foreign. It annoys Americans when people forget dates, or are late to appointments, but it is good to consider that numbers are not always important. Instead, foreign persons value relationships more.

Numbers have a lot to do with winning; winning for most Americans is practically everything. What fails to impress most Americans, is that winning is like a coin, with two (some people believe three) sides: the point is that for each winner, there is a loser. Losing is not a good thing; no one really likes to lose. Losing leaves a bad taste, makes one think that they are not good enough. Winning elevates the individual and/or group that wins, accords them trophies and other stuff, and since there is a hierarch of stuff for winners and losers, winners get all the best stuff and leaves losers sore. Some losers do not lose well.

The idea of winning can be applied to the situation with other countries and other people: in winning, there is often a loser, and generally, if you are in the other person's space and reminding them that they lost, it can go very, very badly for you, the winner. The great obsession with winning, and highlighting how much better America and its people are than the rest of the world is often offensive to the recipients.

One of the major problems with this approach is that while it is true that each country is the best in the world bar all others, believing that the rest of the world is crappy, and rubbing it in their faces is not helpful to the standing of America.

Here is a piece of advice: greatness does not have to be rubbed in the faces of those that are not great. If you are great, you don't need to remind everyone in the room or in the world. It might inflate your ego to the point that you don't notice others' comparative greatness, and if you combine winning with greatness, it becomes purely annoying.

Another way to think of it is this: most basketball players in the NBA are quite tall. Shaquille O'Neal and LeBron James do not have to tell anyone that they are tall, because they are, and everyone knows it. It is implied that in the height category, they reign – and neither they, nor their shorter counterparts, need reminding of their various heights. Ok, that point is totally irrelevant.

Bottom line is this: if you are a great nation, while it is extremely tempting to rub it in everyone else's face, this is generally a bad idea. Mostly because part of your greatness should leverage psychologists to study the "other" and tell you that when there is nothing else to lose, people (and nations) will lose everything – including life. Hate, as much as love, are powerful emotions. Most especially if you are in the other individual's face. America is a great nation. Everyone knows it. It doesn't help to remind everyone of how *not* great they are. It pisses them off. And then they become like the incredible hulk.

But – we digress – there are certain aspects of a great nation that can make it not great, despite what every commercial might say. Let's get to the things that make the country not so great.

Chapter 1
Military Superiority and Competence

One of the most commonly used indicators of a nation's greatness is a country's military power. Without a doubt, the United States spends more on its defense – including for such *illogical* defense expenses as having bases and troops stationed in the largely peaceful, post-war, post-modern Germany – than most other countries combined. It is not clear that this defense spending is directly proportional or reflective of the security that the United States enjoyed, as previously pointed out.

In many respects, some major aspects of history and their implications for how we think about the world have largely bypassed the United States – for example, the fact that the Berlin Wall came crashing down on 11th November 1989, and that the Soviet Union, the United States' arch-enemy, is no more.

Also, while this may not be widely popular or strategically acceptable logic, it absolutely does not make sense to continue to have soldiers stationed in Germany as if Europe is going to fight another land war among its powers – why have the nukes then? Seems one or the other would have sufficed.

Since becoming the greatest nation on earth – and by the way, it is not clear when that happened, since before the Second World War, the United States believed that it had no business in Europe and anywhere else except South America and the Philippines – the world has not necessarily been a better place. And even during its greatness, it has been on the wrong side of history more often than not. When – and after – the United States was finally invited by the Japanese to join the rest of the world, it has made every country and every situation its business, with mixed results. Is this an argument that the United States was better off not involved?

Not hardly. The world is mostly better off, for one hesitates to think of what the world would be like if we all spoke Mandarin and ate rice at every meal (totally insensitive there); arguably, socialism and communism have not done the world a favor and especially due to their ineffectiveness, they have left the world to believe that western government, civilization and democracy are the most viable end-states of man's existence.

Wars

The United States has fought its share of wars since the Second World Wars, including other countries' and peoples' wars (for example, inheriting the "French Mess" in Indochina) and going on to make it the second longest war. True, it is part of the "war on terror" – which by itself is a misnomer, since the essence of war is terror and victory – but that aside, the record of war-fighting and winning for the United States does not inspire confidence.

Most recently, the United States of America has been engaged in several half-hearted attempts at fighting. They are half-hearted, because in addition to asking countries such as Lithuania and Latvia to help fight Iraqis and Afghanis (with due apology to Lithuanians and Latvians and every other small nation), there was a nasty aftertaste due to what was not accomplished.

It is unconscionable that the most powerful nation on earth, with about 100 times the defense expenditure of Afghanistan, can be held at a near-stalemate, nee defeated, by groups of farmers and opium growers with AK-47's, caves and a death wish. [Newsflash: that is the kind of war you never win, so don't even start fighting it unless you want to use another nuclear bomb to flatten the caves].

If the United States has won a war, it is hard to remember when: the last major war it won was the Second World War, against the Japanese, and even then, it wasn't in the traditional fighting sense: for the first and only time in mankind's history, nuclear weapons were used.

Now, this is not to rail against nuclear weapons - the art of war necessitates that you use everything in your arsenal to fight the enemy, rather than line up both sides and see who kills more people, as happened in the US civil war and other wars before it. And that is precisely the reason the United States won; wars are dirty, they are about super-whelming force, and ensuring that the other party never wants to fight again.

The United States of America has won a number of other less-than-reputable "skirmishes" and conflicts; these include Grenada, Panama and Nicaragua, all blips on the map as far as the importance of nations goes. In wars, it is not the *numeric* value of won conflicts that counts; it is the strength of the adversary that counts – also, the quality of the win might come into question. Did the US "lose" in Somalia?

If the United States decides to go to war with a nation that has a smaller population – and territory size – than the state of New York and a thousandth of its defense expenditure, it is not credible to consider that a real military victory. Now, if the United States went to war with Canada, the United Kingdom, China, Russia – or an equally or slightly underwhelming foe, and came out on top, that is a more credible win.

For the troops who fight in these small wars, of course it counts, and the whole nation can then go ahead and chalk up another "win" - even despite the losses that come with such simple combat. A closer examination of many military conflicts that the United States has been involved in will however show that other than in these inconsequential wars and conflicts, the United States *generally* blinks when it comes to a real, almost equally matched adversary.

The United States blinks

Take for example the "great war" that was supremely (over) hyped that when it didn't happen, it was such a collective sigh of disappointment: the 45-year old almost-war between the United States and the Soviet Union. As historians and political scientists will generally argue, there were several wars / skirmishes; it was simply that they were fought as proxy wars: Korea, Vietnam, and Beirut, among others. For forty five years, the two faced each other, with the United States finally managing to stare down the Soviet Union and taking credit for the crumbling of an internal system that was primed to fail anyway.

Of course we will never know what would have happened had the United States actually decided to fight the Soviet Union (remember, during the first part of the Second World War, the Soviet Union was buddy-buddy with the fascists and the Nazis, which seems to me to be a good reason to have fought them). Especially before the Soviet Union stole the "fat man" bomb design; the mere threat of the bomb might have changed the outcome of the end of the war. And the Soviets did not quite know that the United States did not have a fourth bomb, neither did they have the recipe for the bomb.

Instead, the United States blinked at the most critical point, allowing half of modern Europe's population to live under communism / socialism for a generation. The greatest war, therefore, was the one that was never fought. When the opportunities came to re-fight that particular war - for example, in Cuba, 1962 - it was too late and too dangerous: the Soviets already had the (stolen) bomb and had taken the lead in the space race.

Now, it might be argued that for example, during the Second World War, the United States won a great victory, but let's face it: the United States really fought one and two halves of a country: Germany and Italy. Admittedly, the

United States fought Japan all the way from Hawaii to Tokyo, and the Italians in North Africa and Germans from Normandy to Berlin.

This is how I conceptualize the war against Germany: think of a farmer who goes into the forest to cut down a tree - for whatever use. Picks on one of the biggest trees, and with his axe, hacks away at it, taking some breaks, some rest, and some breathers. Just about halfway, he is almost tiring, and his friend comes along, picks up the axe, and starts chipping away at the already weakened tree.

France took a lot of the blunt of the blitzkrieg, and the bombing of London - with the process reversed when the Brits started cross-channel raids, the opposition in France and in the occupied territories - made quite a difference.

When the United States came along, all refreshed, the "tree-cutting" by the Brits and the French had taken a toll on the Germans, who were both desperate and on the run. True, the United States helped very much, but credit where credit is due; it should be shared by the Brits and the French. And some of it can be attributed to the British-recruited Kings African Rifles.

The United States has blinked – and lost against other less formidable adversaries. Take for instance the now infamous *Black Hawk Down*. The United States lost against a bunch of street urchins with guns and unshakeable, irredeemable death wishes, but ably commanded by a general-turned-warlord. This most probably put a dent in the United States' tale of greatness, considering that at the time, it had balked from fighting the next greatest army – several million or so – of the Soviet Union. How do the greatest country's most elite soldiers lose to a bunch of ragheads armed with AK-47's and a death wish?

What comes to mind immediately is Tomahawk cruise missiles, drones, cluster bombs and the question: why on earth wouldn't you leverage all the resources of the United States Armed Forces to extract the troops and/or revenge for Black Hawk Down? *Complexity*. The United States sometimes complicates matters more than they need to be. But I digress.

In fact, why would the greatest country on earth sit by and watch while a third-rate power such as Ethiopia, thrice, and Kenya, once, went in and kicked out the terrorists, Islamists and other shades of Al Shabaab and stabilize the country without claiming greatness, and with 1960's technology and fewer casualties than the United States? Especially after they sent the said greatest country scurrying and killed a whole bunch of its soldiers?

Take Libya, for instance, 1986. Clearly, there was an attribution of the bombing of the Berlin Disco hall with deaths of American servicemen to Libya. The argument for exacting revenge was compelling: but why do it half-heartedly? A few F-111's with bunker-busting bombs? Really, the greatest nation on earth could have learnt from the lessons and example of one of their greatest allies: Israel.

You see, Israel generally shunned taking any prisoners most of the time: they destroy the enemy (as Amin came to find out in Entebbe, 1977) and as the Egyptians found out when they discovered that they did not have an Air Force because the Israelis had done the militarily sensible thing and destroyed it on the ground. Had Reagan borrowed (albeit in the future) Bill Clinton's example, he would have sent cruise missiles to destroy the Libyan Air Force defenses, much as George Bush would later do with the First Gulf War, and his son would do in the second, and then flattened Libya. Okay, maybe proportional response is much overrated.

The point of this is that the United States has rarely won any conflicts in which it has engaged in, at least without the help of others. Gulf War One was a coalition - but really, even if it had not been, what would Iraq have done? Park the ships in the Gulf of Aden and the Mediterranean and Red Sea and unleash the power of "shock and awe"

For future reference, the lessons of the past might be

useful, and they would most decidedly have advanced the legend of greatness. When you go to war, look and act as if you are going to war, be decisive, remember that war is about taking out the threat and ensuring that the other guy/gal has no appetite to fight in future. Also, ensure that after the fight/war is over, there is no doubt who, as the Americans would say, is the top dog, and the opponent is so thoroughly put in his place that they lose the appetite for fighting (remember Japan? Ok, the Japanese might not like the reference to them, but he idea worked quite well, still does). And quit sharing the victory with the Kyrgyz Republic.

Also, running from a few Somali would-in-future-become pirates after losing 18 elite rangers on the streets is in bad form, as these things go (learn from the Russians in Afghanistan) and the French in Algeria. Take revenge. Bomb a rebel camp, target a warlord.

Also: fight with spirit. The greatest nation on earth does not run from Somalia, if for nothing else, pride and an example to others. Running from a fight gives other nations and ragtag militia the wrong idea: they will be trying to make you do it again, especially since they generally have nothing to lose.

One of the biggest constraints in fighting is the propensity to take cameras along. It is not clear what value the cameras add to a fight, other than ensuring that the victory is not total. War, with media 'embedded', becomes more of an exercise in obtaining good footage for a movie rather than getting the proper job done. And one might learn ere from their enemies: one never saw the Taliban with cameras as they try to get the better of some American unit out at the caves.

The propensity for drama has permeated the serious business of war and turned it into a day at the circus. Instead of actually carrying on with the business of war, war becomes an extension of the American sense of entertaining the masses in practically everything. Cameras and the media do not belong anywhere near or in wars. They should be left in Hollywood, entertaining the public.

Choosing wrong, no support

The United States has another dubious distinction: that of fighting practically all the wrong wars, and ignoring the wars it should fight. And worse, the insulation to criticism does not much help it to consider whether the wars are justified or not, and whether it ought to exercise more caution in choosing the wars it fights.

Take the "on-going" Korean War. Involvement with South Korea, which while now a valuable ally, was based on the flawed premise of understanding geo-politics, and the notion of containing the advancement of communism everywhere born out of the Long Telegram and the Marshall Plan.

In retrospect, what would have been the tragedy of South Korea falling to communist rule? South Korea was one more country, several thousand miles away from the United States, not an existential threat to the national security of the United States. True, it may be now living in the shadow of the Great Leader, Kim Jong Un, but at what point should the United States stop worrying about communism?

After all, the United States watched while the United Kingdom gave back Hong Kong to Communist China without intervening. And, the citizens of a country have the right to decide the kind of government they want. If one really wants to help, drones could be put to really good use.

After the Korean debacle, the United States decided to get even more deeply mired in the jungles of Asia, by taking on the French Mess in Indochina, which I am certain the French were only too glad to hand over to somebody. [In fairness: the French do not learn well – they are French, after all – and went ahead to get involved in a dirty war in Algeria, one they would lose badly.]

So the United States inherited Viet Nam, a bad war that should never have been the United States' business, a fact of which should have been clear simply by sitting down with Ho Chi Minh. He had been explaining – and one might add, since the abortive League of Nations – that Viet Nam was not about communism.

Rather, it was the idea of self-determination, of freedom, of independence, and of throwing out the French. Ho Chi Minh was going to get the French out – with or without American help. It was not going to be the last time that the Americans read a situation wrong (the Somalia collapse of Central Government into fiefdoms, tribes and clans was read all wrong by US State Department and most of US government).

The United States has shown great proclivity towards choosing the *wrong wars*. It also goes on to lose the wrongly chosen wars, which have an additional consequence: the lack of support among friends, allies and even the populations where she finds herself often fighting.

America's wars and staying power

The United States' record of winning wars is dismal, even though it has initiated and/or been involved in about 60 conflicts, military actions and other armed interventions over the past century or so. The United States has neither the stomach for, nor the staying power, to wage wars and to win in conflicts – perhaps mainly because it is difficult to justify American interest in many of them.

The process of declaring wars – through the War Powers Act which practically every president since Nixon has ignored – makes declaring war and/or entering hostilities a very interesting process. In other countries, you just go to war, you don't go through protracted votes and hearings and incessant justifications for fighting or not fighting, with everyone – including the ill-informed – opining.

This, unfortunately, exposes most of the public to the

process of war-fighting. When you add Almond's mood theory into the mix, it becomes quite evident that there are few conflicts that have unanimous or simply overwhelming support to fight; indeed, it is difficult to find one that had such, except perhaps the "war on terror".

Quite shortly after the onset of hostilities, the "drive-thru mentality" takes over: one can expect the support for war to be limited to all of three months. After that, it is simply taking too long. Even then, the first few days are simply left to the Air Force and the Navy to destroy opposing infrastructure, before the boots get on the ground; after the boots get on the ground, two months is generally a goodish length for expectations for a win (there we go again).

Casualties are something that Americans – especially the public – does not take well. This is not to argue that anyone should take casualties well, or fight to find out how they take casualties, but study of major wars may show how well, as one professor put it "Russians know how to die well" especially in conflict. This was especially well illustrated during World War II.

Americans did take casualties "fairly well" during World War II, Korea and Vietnam, but after that, the appetite for war and attendant casualties began to diminish. The Iraq II war had casualties numbering about 4,500. For such a protracted war, that was quite a low number of casualties (compare to the Vietnam War, the Korean War or even World War II).

In short, Americans no longer have the patience, the tolerance or the stomach for fighting what might be considered conventional wars, which often come with high body counts. This may be a good thing, because it is useful in helping restrict the number of conflicts that the United States initiates, especially given its military capabilities. In other words, a bully with a conscience – even if that is driven by fear of casualties – is a good bully.

Everything is not a movie

Movies are useful, in that they allow for one to create a situation they can control. Wars are rarely that way: one does not always get the outcome they want (case in point: Iraq and Afghanistan). The outcome may have been informed by the method of fighting, and the limits to which the United States was willing to go.

Wars are not movies: the greatest fighting machine in the world has often been put to severe test by bands of poorly armed rebels (Vietnam), ragtag militia (Somalia), insurgents (Afghanistan and Iraq) and other less-than-reputable fighting units. In movies, it is plausible for Van Damme to fight an entire army by with just a band comparable to the *expendables*, but wars are often dirty, long, drawn-out affairs that need gravitas, staying power and a ruthlessness often seen in movies but rarely practised in real life.

It does not help to fight wars as if they were a movie shoot. Naturally, the screams of "collateral damage" will accompany the reading of this section; Japan did produce quite a bit of collateral damage, as did Germany, but look at the present outcome.

Superior technology and wargaming

More importantly, war is not a game. True, there are exercises in war games, using all kinds of technology, but why not use it all the way? The essence of fighting is to overwhelm the other side in a way that leaves no doubt who the top-dog is. In that sense, use of technology is nothing to be ashamed of; in fact, it may allow for more wins with fewer casualties.

Consider perhaps the earliest wars in the history of mankind. It is fair to suggest that since there were no weapons (unless you consider rocks, flints and bone fragments to be weapons) fists were used – and it is exceedingly difficult to kill anyone using fists unless you are a boxer or an MMA fighter. Technology has grown –

from fist to flint, musket to missile, bomb to drone, and there is no shame in using either and/or all of these tools to win. Advances in technology should make war never necessary because the outcome is not in doubt.

As the self-identified greatest nation on earth, it is important to act like it. Use the superior technology to smoke out insurgents from caves, and then drone them back onto the stone-age. And stop worrying so much about casualties; in wars, that is what happens; fighters, soldiers and civilians die. Use the superior technology, destroy the enemy, and don't leave the outcome in doubt. In other words, fight wars like wars are meant to be fought.

Chapter 2
An emotional people

Emotionally, Americans are some of the most needy, almost weak individuals anyone has ever met. Either that, or the medical industry, its paymaster, the pharmaceutical industry, in cahoots with the media, are extremely clever and determined to medicate everyone they can, based on some notion of a need for some psychological adjustment.

Take the mental health issues that folks routinely have. It is probably impossible for a therapist to meet anyone whom they could not diagnose with some mental health illness or some maladjustment. This is how the United States compares to other places in terms of "normal: if you hold up your thumb and index finger, and separate them as far as possible, that is the spectrum for normal. For the rest of the world, hold up both arms as far as they will go: that is the level of normal for everyone.

Neural, emotional and psychological adjustment (or mental health issues) and attendant behavioral disorders in this society are caused by practically everything: absence of, temporal and or permanent parental abandonment – even where the parent would be a negative force on the child; a parent going to work (called separation anxiety), poor lighting in the winter (seasonal adjustment disorder) – and a host of other disorders. This inability to deal with life results in a disproportionate number of Americans being in some sort of therapeutic care.

Americans are simply incapable of dealing with the simplest of life's natural occurrences and need "interventions" and therapy to deal with ordinary life. A break-up or divorce from a spouse, death of a family member – are fixed with "grief counseling", to "cope" with what one is going through. What is one supposed to do when their heart is broken, go out and throw a party? (Okay, that may be a plan, especially if the person was full of dung). Of course they will be sad for a while, and then they will get over it and move on. It is called the natural order of things. There is no need to get that person to pop pills or anything.

Psychiatrists and other types of therapists appear to hold the American society hostage: they are wont to diagnose practically everyone with some type of "issue." Since the scope of "normal" is so restricted, it is very easy for an individual to attract a diagnosis, even when they do not need one. Now, this is not to dismiss some severely ill-adjusted persons: there are mental health issues out there, and some of them are quite severe. But it is not evident that they are more prevalent in the United States more than they are in other countries. Hint: talk to your grandmother/father! They are (used to be) the best therapists around!

Some of what constitutes "mental health issues" or behavioral disorders are really kids locked up in air-conditioned houses, with nothing to do, being kids. What kid does not get into a few scrapes when they are growing up? And if they shove each other around a little on the playground, that is perfectly ok. The problem with the United States is that guns have replaced fists, and instead of settling the problems on the playground by fists, it goes to the next level, and even what begins as shoving each other around the playground may later be the impetus for something more disturbing.

One diagnosis of the problems of children's behavior is lack of open spaces to play. Because society has also failed to observe simple standards of conduct, including allowing kids to play outside (wait, there is no outside – it is all mostly concrete) and parents worrying every minute that their child will get hurt, kids are locked up all day in the house and this makes for too much energy (in addition to eating too many cookies at all times of day) and no outlet; they begin punching holes in walls and voila! They get a diagnosis.

Emotionally, Americans are quite the sissies. Simple issues such as the trauma of military deployments are overhyped. They are filled with moments of drama and explanations of how devastating their experience is. The media is helpful in playing out this drama: they will interview everyone – even folks who have no investment in the goings-on, to get their perspective about how they would feel if their loved ones were being deployed.

The experience then traumatizes and re-traumatizes the citizens and the viewers, inculcating belief that a high level of trauma is the appropriate reaction to have. Why, some lady was "traumatized" because her car did not have sufficient traction while she was driving over snow that had iced over after a 2-inch snowfall!

The American society can be quite unbelievable in the handling of grief and trauma. It is true that some events are quite traumatic, but is also not clear that these are not capable of being handled easily and overcoming the consequences with which they come. The media makes a whole show of revisiting the issues, succeeding in not only extracting every ounce of drama from a single event – until the next event – and re-traumatizing the said victims.

Man-made disasters

There is an African saying, which goes something like this: "self-inflicted grief attracts no sympathy". It is a stretch to suggest that no one should feel devastated by natural phenomena such as hurricanes and earthquakes, but one wonders why, knowing the potential for such calamity does not provoke even better preparations (building shelters, better, stone houses, warning systems) to reduce the impact of the disasters on peoples' lives.

The capacity to deal with natural disasters, which are as frequent as the days on the calendar, is quite minimal. There is a particular fatalism about the American people that makes them want to contest nature, which is quite an unwinnable prospect. The *tornado alley* is one place that perhaps one should be careful about making a home, and if the home is sucked up in a tornado, oh well, what did one expect? Of course CNN and every other local affiliate will be there to cover it. *Fatalism.*

Some might argue that this fatalism and its attendant incapacity to deal with adversity is mostly, and especially pronounced, among the WASP populations of the country. After all, the Black American part of America has been dealing with insurmountable adversity for close on four hundred years and actually, has only *not* dealt with adversity for all of sixty years. Other minorities have also been stoic about dealing with their share of adversity, sometimes inflicted by the WASP section of the United States: Mexicans have been invaded, classified "wetbacks", disliked, deported and in other ways, been made unwelcome. So have the Japanese, Italians, Irish, Chinese, Africans and Native Americans. Adversity improves stoicism.

Capacity for adversity

There is overall a diminished capacity among most of the American public to withstand adversity. There is a mental; a psychological weakness among the general publics that makes them unable to withstand even the most easily manageable issues relating to emotional strength and ability to persevere and thrive when "normal" gets upset. Americans have generally discarded the traditional systems that used to manage such issues and now unseasonably rely on their doctors, therapists and pills to manage life.

They have discarded the naturalistic healing of the mind and soul, the great conversation with the grandmother that sets emotions and expectations right. They have come to expect emotions to work with precision such as is found in their electrical systems or road grids. They have failed to recognize the dissimilarity between emotions and mechanics. While they feel too much, display too much emotion, their emotions are sand castles; they crumble quickly and rely on expert systems to tell them what they should feel, how they should feel and how they should conduct their emotions.

The capacity to overcome pain, hurt and other unexpected outcomes in life is highly diminished. It makes them weak, it constantly changes the "normal' and creates a permanent class of individuals who are less than normal. It creates an emotionally weak society, one incapable of the strength of leadership demanded by a future world. Summarized: Americans are emotional weaklings.

Chapter 3
Politics of a great nation

The United States is considered a constitutional republic with representative government: that is, the people elect their representatives to Congress, the House of Representatives and the Senate, which are the law-making bodies. It also has a judicial system and an executive, comprising of the President and a Cabinet.

Since its inception, the United States has prided itself to have been continuously democratic (never mind the limits imposed at certain points in its history, including close to the current, close to 4 million persons incarcerated and whose voting rights are often constrained). The question of whether it has continuously been a democracy is one to contemplate especially when one considers that women could not vote until 1920, and blacks did not have the right to vote until about 1965.

The world has known, and there are still many atrocious political systems, which generally limit participation, rights, freedoms, or trample over them. Some are based on religious belief or tradition; others are based on concepts of human rights. The United States is somewhat unique in this respect, founded on Christian principles, but increasingly becoming secular.

As the United States has progressively found, it is very difficult to impose a political system on any other country. People have to want to change; of special importance is the knowledge of what people value most. In the United States, it is plausible to believe that most people value individual rights; in Saudi Arabia, people probably value their relationships with their clansmen and tribesmen over their individual rights.

The individualist orientation of the American society makes its particular brand of democracy possible; in countries such as Tanzania, where "brotherhood" is more important, or many other countries where kinship is more pronounced, individual rights may not be as important or the founding blocks of politics.

Politically Ineffective

The United States' political system is one to marvel, mostly for what it was intended to *not* do. Careful study of the Articles of the Confederacy, the Constitutional Convention and the subsequent explanatory Federalist Papers paint the picture of a rather confused system: neither King, nor commoner, neither royalty nor parliamentary. The checks and balances are dizzying and extremely effective in their contribution to gridlock.

Take for example, declaration of war. The president is the Commander in Chief of the Army and the Navy (curiously, the Constitution did not mention and/or envisage the Air Force; one would think this might have been inserted somewhere through a constitutional amendment). If and when hostilities are declared, the generals report to the C-in-C.

But.

Congress appropriates funds for the army and the navy and for most other government functions. So, technically, the President could declare war on a foreign land, but congress could refuse to appropriate funds to pay for the war. It is an important distinction, because if there was a dictatorial leader, then it would be more difficult to stop them from constantly declaring wars and paying for them, especially since they would be able have the means to fund the wars.

Presidents went ahead and declared wars anyway, which

royally infuriated congress, which eventually took some action: the War Powers Act of 1973 was meant to ensure that Presidents would not declare war without Congressional approval. Nixon, predictably, vetoed the legislation, a veto that was overridden by Congress.

Yet, there has not been serious enforcement of the War Powers Act, mostly because any president can send troops into a conflict and then tighten the screws on Congress by leveraging public opinion: who wants to leave troops out in the field without pay, logistics and other support? It would be political suicide.

The United States is fond of referring back to certain aspects of its founding: most conservatives are firmly embedded in the constitution. What is amazing is that there is an almost glossing-over of the parts that no one likes. It is unfathomable that on the one hand, the nation would be inseparably wedded to the constitution – the very same one whose interpretation did not allow for blacks and women – at least originally – to be considered full citizens of the United States. It is not clear how these disconnects are addressed.

Fallacy of democracy

Democracy is not always, or necessarily, the best system of government for everyone. In fact, it is exceedingly difficult to make pure democracy work (at least, in most places other than Switzerland). The United States' democratic model is not replicable in many other places. It is characterized by a lot of issues; from corruption to political dynasties, gridlock to too many laws (hence the great number of its citizens in prison).

Democracy assumes that people have the same desire for the same types of freedoms. What ever happened to the notion that "what you don't know cannot hurt you"? The North Koreans have never had representative government; it is possible that they would not know what to do with it. Also, it is not clear why there would be an assumption that all people want democracy, or that all countries can flourish under democracy.

What one needs to figure out is this: what do people value? Does the Muslim woman who covers up all her body and just leaves a space for the eyes feel oppressed just because she does not have a choice to take it all off? What would happen if she took off the coverings – the *hijab or the burqa* and no one in the village talked to her because she would now be ostracized?

You see, democracy requires for a society to be very individualistic. Collectivist societies are driven more by the need to belong. Now, granted, the ability to choose one's future life is extremely important, but if you are the socially ostracized member of a small farming community in Irbil, simply because you chose to express your preferences (the notion of democracy over community), you are likely to find yourself without any friends or suitors. At that point, democracy begins to lose its allure. One is reminded of the Zambians, when told about democracy and multi-party politics. They are reported to have asked if they were going to "eat" democracy. You have to appreciate that Zambians were more interested in eating than in democracy.

Suffice to say, democracy is good when it works. But again, the essence of democracy is the ability to choose. When the Palestinians chose Hamas in 2005, the United States especially was rather unamused. It began to appear that democracy worked when it produced the outcomes that you wanted it to produce, not the ones that it produced.

Democracy is about choices, the opportunities to make them, even the choices that you don't like. The aggregation of those choices leads to ensuring the majority decision is implemented. But if there are only two major choices, how democratic is that? The two major parties in the US point to this phenomenon…it is not clear that US democracy is better than India's with its more than 300 political parties.

Gridlock and law-making

For the level of political gridlock that it experiences, it is impressive the number of laws that are on the book in the United States. Partisanship in the politics of the United States is at an all-high, with the party-line voting being the highest it has been in the history of the country.

It is almost accepted that there are two major political parties in the US: the Democrats and the Republicans. Of course, there are fringe parties, such as the Party of Rent is Too Damn High, the Greens, and I am quite certain there are a few communists somewhere in the country. The question is why the acceptance of two parties is near universal: third-party candidates rarely make it to win seats (actually, the only other candidates who have won office have mainly been Independents).

India has more than 300 political parties. Granted, it is practically impossible to have 300 different ideologies and political planks that are uniquely different, and this seems to be quite some overkill. Still, there aren't just two different ideologies, and it appears that in the US, the electors have to compromise in the selection of candidates that represent all their possible preferences.

Some aspects of the American political system are simply bewildering. Take the Electoral College, which has significant national support and which in effect elects the President of the United States. Ok, that is where the complication comes in. Citizens vote for Representatives and Senators. They also vote for the Presidential Candidate. Yet, technically, they are voting for the Electors (members of the Electoral College), who will then elect the President. In two states, Maine and Nebraska, the states divide the Electoral College Votes but most other states award them to the candidate winning the most popular votes. So, why the Electors? Hmmm….

Well, when the United States was still a very young country, the founding 'fathers' were concerned that allowing every other Tom, Dick and Harry to vote – and yes, it was only Tom, Dick and Harry who were initially allowed to vote; Sue, Betty and Jane were not – allowing them to vote would expose the country to leadership that was elected by farmers, regular folks and commoners and it did not bode well for the elites to have that happen.

So they figured that a select group of 'well-informed' citizens who could scrutinize the character of the candidates for president and (sometimes overriding the wishes of the citizens), elect the person most suited to the Presidency. Now, if that is not the height of elitism, it is not clear what is.

So the Electoral College, institutionalized in the constitution, became one of the hallmarks of the electoral process. Never mind that after 1840's, voting was opened up from the exclusive club of land-owners to salon and inn-keepers, bar-keeps and every other *adult male*. The Electoral College did not change much, and it has gone on to do some obvious damage to the election of the President (1896 and 2000 are very good examples).

[Newsflash for the United States: for the record, everyone that was not physically present in the United States in 2000 was collectively shocked at the outcome and the fact that the election was obviously stolen – the United States resembled Zimbabwe, Russia or Italy for a moment].

Congressional Terms

One of the points of disagreement with the King of England that led to the *Mayflower* departing England so long ago, was the lack of accountability by the King, since he was not elected (technically, he believed that God elected him). The King did not feel answerable to anyone, so the King did as the King wished.

To curtail that, the newly constituted United States were going to have term limits for the new regent (president), which were steeped in tradition that was first established by George Washington by serving two terms.

There are Congressmen and Senators who have served up to fifty six years. While they are not the president, it is not significantly different from the depots of the Middle East who often serve forty years with no constraints or consequences. There are kids who were born, and grew up to become adults, knowing John Dingell as their Congressman and with no chance that he might give up the political class label.

Stuff does not always work as planned – in fact, Murphy's Law has often seen to that. The notion of abolishing the "political class", folks who would always be in Washington conducting the business of the people, was well intentioned; however, Congress has become an occupation. It does not hurt that all one has to do is have a platform, a clean record, convince enough people to give enough money to buy ads trashing the other guy(s) and girl(s) and get elected – and then get re-elected, endlessly.

Government and the people
It has always been amazing how much the people do not, and almost have never, trusted government. In the recent years, it has become clear whey. Government is not always benevolent. Government can, in fact, be actively evil. It is government that allowed for the appropriation of the land from the Indians, allowed the Homestead Act to go on, and incarcerated Japanese American citizens.

The business of the United States government – especially that of the Congress – seems to be mainly to make new laws, to find ways to tax people more, starve poor citizens, enrich richer citizens and hate on immigrants. Per capita, the United States probably has more laws on the books than any other country on earth. These laws, while intended to protect people from one thing or another, including from each other and from themselves, but it is most probable that on any given day, even well-meaning citizens break a few hundred laws, mainly because they don't know the laws, or the laws make practically no sense.

For instance, in many cities in the Commonwealth of Virginia, it is against the law to have sex in any position other than the "missionary" position. Who regulates what position one has sex in, without infringing on privacy, or are individuals expected to snitch on themselves? The laws date from a while ago, but at some point they should be reconsidered.

The US government, through its very many agencies, has made it its business the business of the people. Some of the most hated branches of government include the Internal Revenue Service, the IRS. While universally hated, the citizens rarely do anything to curtail its influence. One wonders what ever happened to the patriots who brewed ice (or at least cold) tea in the Boston Harbor to protest British rule and taxation without representation. One would think that at some point, there would be some collective *angst* that would lead the people to protest agencies such as the IRS.

The tragedy of government is that it quickly and often dangerously outgrows its role. As modern events have shown, governmental agencies such as the NSA often far exceed their constitutional and legislated roles and become behemoths that cannot be controlled. They actively begin threatening the very citizens for whom they are established to protect.

This is the growing negative role of government. Often, citizens are cowed by the articulation of such threats as terrorism, and even where their personal freedoms are threatened, they are too afraid to actually articulate their distaste for what government often becomes or does to their lives. And yet, ironically, the citizens of the great nation still believe that they have freedoms, which are often excused by the notion that if one is not doing anything wrong, they have nothing to fear from government agencies such as the CIA, the NSA, DEA or the FBI.

But who is to decide that one day, the government will not decide that it is their business to determine the level of morality – if they discover for instance that one is having a "take-out" affair, should not determine the level of government intrusion? It is the principle, not the function that the government puts the information that it collects to use. Americans appear resigned to allow the very instruments designed to protect them to become too powerful and do not realize that this is how police states are born.

The people and the law

First off, there comes a time in every country's life when it must determine that its citizens are a reasonable, intelligent peoples, who can take a leak in a bathroom without requiring a law (with a financial disincentive) to make sure they don't do so in the woods. Tragically, the United States has not evolved to that level, mostly because of the lack of community – and the focus on individuality.

There are way too many laws on way too many books for any average citizen of these United States to know, keep track of and avoid violating. The business of Congress, it appears, is to regulate everything. Americans appear to be unable to make even the simplest decisions. They cannot decide which way to park without having signs telling them where to park, which way their car should face, where the parking zone begins, how to drive through the parking lot (i.e., whether they can drive through a parking lot or not), where to fish (or not) – for example, on a bridge…

On any given day, even law abiding citizens break a few hundred laws, in part due to ignorance of their existence, and in part due to the fact that they are contrary to common sense. The police generally may arrest the worst offenders, but it is quite difficult to catch someone spitting on the side-walk. These are some of the situations that ought to be regulated by common sense.

The existence of the laws is often unknown by the said citizens. This can be well illustrated by one of the most contentious recent legislation: the Affordable Care Act, where one of the Democratic Congressional leaders suggested that the other party pass the legislation and *then* they would get to know what was in the legislation. It appears that every time Congress meets, it finds a way to generate new laws. Why, at this rate, we might pretty soon regulate where Canadian geese fly and stick them in jail if they don't comply!

American society rarely fights these laws. There is an almost hopeless resignation to the fact that most of the citizens cannot affect change and live under the sometimes dumb laws. Only when the laws have financial consequences do citizens appear to be agitated enough to want to do something about it. On average, most Americans are content to blindly follow the law, however dumb it is, without as much as questioning the law's intent, meaning, purpose or effectiveness.

A sissy people

Of course, Americans do occasionally mount half-hearted protests – between their email and internet and other things that run their lives. However, they do so without vigor, and without the sustained type of *angst* and determination that has been witnessed in countries such as Egypt, Libya, Tunisia, Ukraine or Greece. The protests Americans engage in include such as those that were witnessed during the Vietnam War, or during the Civil Rights Movement.

Over time, Americans have lost the gravitas needed to insure their freedoms, which have been gradually eroded by government without much protest from the citizens. On paper, and even in real life, Americans can protest, but because their government has been sufficiently smart to provide at least the basic freedoms and the semblance of the citizens having freedoms to pursue happiness, the government's shortcomings and infringements on citizens' rights are seen as less severe and often attributed to individuals' lack shortcomings.

The last major rounds of protests that impacted the welfare of Americans, over issues that redefine society in ways similar to the Middle Eastern and former Soviet Union countries were during the Civil Rights era. Of course, this may mean that American democracy has come of age, and that there are not significant issues over which to protest. Or, it might just mean that Americans have given up on challenging the power of government.

Chapter 4
Social relations

"The air-conditioner and the remote control together conspired to kill the American society"

No, I did not quote anyone; this is my firm belief. Past the fact that it is not clear why the founders decided to inhabit a continent that oscillated from one end of hot to the other end of cold, rather than, say, inhabiting Africa which is naturally air-conditioned, "progress", while great, sounded – this relates to the future – the death knell for the American society.

Consider this: a few hundred (or maybe not that many) years ago, most people did not have air conditioning. So when it was cold, they would crowd around a fire, drink vodka (ask the Russians) and tell stories (okay, maybe they did not). In such circumstances, inevitably, people would begin to talk to each other. When the weather got nicer, everyone would go out – well, most everyone – and enjoy the nice weather since they were sick and tired of having been indoors all winter. So they would have occasion to socialize and form community.

During the summer months, when it got too hot inside, when there was no air-conditioning, to cool down one would have had to go outside – sit on the stoop or on the porch – and the other nosy neighbors would say nice things to them, thus making sure that some socialization was going on.

Then some genius invented the air conditioner, or the A/C. With A/C, it was entirely possible to sit inside the house for days on end, and have no compunction to go share a fire (how primitive), seeing as one was warm and did not need to crowd around the communal fire. As such, it began to be possible to avoid conversation with the neighbors – whom one may not like anyway – and the same thing would happen in the summer. It was possible to be cooler inside, so there was less motivation or need to be outdoors.

Then came *The Tube*. Not *that* tube; the Television. TV. Of course there were many things that were good with the TV; it brought about the whole notion of entertainment *with pictures*, news and so on so much closer. One did not have to wait for the newspaper tomorrow, or use their imagination to figure out what might have gone on, especially when they heard the news on the radio (wait, I didn't even consider that TV killed imagination – you could see the entire thing on TV, who needed imagination?).

The ability to be disconnectedly connected – one was connected to the world outside via the TV, in that they knew what was going on, and yet had the option to shut the world out by a simple click of a button – became more pronounced. With a bunch of programs to watch, was decidedly a very, very attractive option, except for the negatives therein. Now, the illusion was complete. Turn the A/C on, turn the TV on, and it was entirely possible to be disconnected from the rest of the world.

Problematic

Of course this may imply the life of a single individual; families continued to thrive, but needed to do more to spend time together. So the notion of dinner together at the dinner table became more important, as did spending time together doing something "family" oriented. Un/fortunately, TV required more creativity on the part of the broadcasters, so movies, horror movies, family shows that promoted sometimes impossible reality became more widespread. As did the problems they occasioned.

Imagine a child, who might watch TV shows that showed happy families, where the dad spent a bunch of time fishing and playing all kinds of games with their children, and the particular child was not getting the same kind of attention. Without the recognition of the difference in the situation – the reality versus the dramatic – it was entirely possible that the viewing child was having worse outcomes and would be more likely to become a candidate for therapy for lack of proper social adjustment.

The American society thus began reaping the benefits of progress: progress is not always a good thing. Society was exposed to more opportunities for divergence from "normal" due to the inability of some of its members to separate reality from fantasy and the rising instances of "not normal". This gave rise to all kinds of need to deal with the divergence from societal expectations. It was illustrative of how to create a problem and then rue that there was a problem.

Narrow Normal

This is an exercise in stretching fingers. If you, the reader, held up your thumb and forefinger, and separated them as far as possible, that illustrates the extent of "normal" according to the American society. Now, if you stretch your arms – both of them – as far wide as they will go, that illustrates how the rest of the world conceives of "normal".

Of course this is not a scientific exercise. It is one borne of experience, and the rather cozy relationship between the pharmaceutical companies in these United States and the doctors whose single zeal is to find something wrong with everyone. The American public shares in the interest in finding something wrong with them. It is almost as if being normal is abnormal.

It is very rare to find an individual who is healthy, well adjusted, and who does not have "issues". When a couple breaks up, there is generally need for therapy, to "deal with feelings". It is almost as if being human is an anomaly; it is always a condition to be cured. On the other hand, the French are the masters of *feelings*. Whether it be *l'amour*, grief, happiness, flirtation – ok, I am picking on the French. After all, they kind of lost both World War I and II. And the Algerian war of independence. And also lost (but cleverly handed over) Vietnam to the Americans.

The point here is that more Americans are diagnosed with the inability to cope with their environment, per capita, than the citizens in any other country. Perhaps this sort of reflects the zeal of the medical community or perhaps Americans in general have more problems than the citizens of the rest of the world. Whichever the case may be, Americans are generally more prone to mental health diagnoses than the rest of the world. Part of this could be in how they interact with each other and with their environments.

Socially Isolated

Social interaction is extremely important. Human beings are social beings; and socialization does not mean interacting with the Television and through social media. When one travels to some foreign countries, they find different types of interactions among members of society.

For example, if one wants to go see their mother, they don't have to call ahead. The same is true with friends: when one needs to see their friends, you drop in on them. If they are home, that becomes the plan. In these United States, it has become necessary to call ahead to "make plans". You show up, and that is the plan.

Overall, Americans are more isolated than citizens of other countries. It appears that the whole individualism has been taken to another level; community often feels and appears to be a bad concept. Excessive individuality is not always helpful, because then one runs into the problem of being social; one even needs to be taught social skills. That would not be as necessary if people spoke to others.

American society has somehow convinced itself that it is possible to regulate every aspect of life through reward and punishment. Unfortunately, this leaves very little space for the actual spontaneous human interactions. For such a great nation with some of the highest indicators - highest rates of education and such - why is there a need to regulate how and where people use bathrooms? Society ought to be able to determine that taking a leak on the side of a building or in plain view of, say, children, ought to have social consequences (such as being shunned by your neighbors).

But since it is a very individualistic society, the sense of community destroyed (by the remote and A/C), then the social costs of not conforming with norms that ought to be regulated by society falls back to law-enforcement. And gives those folks who are prone to wanting to do something wrong an impetus to try, since they can get away with it considering that the law does not have eyes everywhere. It is important to trust your citizens enough to know that they can form societies and communities with self-regulating mechanisms to ensure that people are not doing stuff they should not do, because their friends will frown upon it, and because it is the right thing to do, rather than because they will get a ticket.

The notion of isolation is taken further to include the previously mentioned "undesirables." American society is very stratified: it is divided by class, even though it prides itself on being equal and having equal opportunities for everyone. Indeed, individuals from low income families are very, very unlikely to pull themselves by their bootstraps.

There are very specific patterns of interaction, and depending on whatever class one is born into. Individuals with mental health issues (some of these issues are environmental, brought on by the choices individuals make - for example, smoking crack) are very isolated, in group homes, independent living facilities and such.

It is unconscionable for most people in especially

developing countries to place their older kin in these group homes or other places where they are closed off and unwanted. The practice is to respect these older folks for their wisdom, not to "throw them away" and hide them out of public viewing.

The United States has perfected the art of "throwing away" socially undesirable people, who form their little islands of isolation in the group homes and other such facilities. Here, the old, the poor, the crazy and all other undesirables are left to form communities, often graced with one visit a year, for a few hours, and mostly left to play bingo or do other stuff that folks in those isolated places do.

Growing old and losing one's mind in such a society is almost a verifiable path to social isolation. There are few older people who remain in their homes, because their relatives are too busy being busy to take care of them. This further impacts and contributes to the social isolation of older and the infirm, and it is clearly not a very healthy practice for those concerned.

There is need to allow for normal human relations to take place, and to stop trying too hard to regulate every aspect of life and contributing to more misery for the older and the infirm, and even the social aspects of their lives. People, when left to their devices, are perfectly capable of making good choices, stable relationships and can vastly improve the social relationships among society members.

Chapter 5
The Economy & Economic system

It boasts what might be considered the most "successful" economic system in modern history. It is an economic system that produces multi-millionaires, billionaires and paupers who work for them. Yet, criticism of the system is often considered criticism of "hard work" and determination, "playing by the rules" and all that claptrap.

Perhaps there have been no other systems that have been similarly successful. Because Americans are uncritical and frequently exhibit the steeple mentality, rather than question the foundations, assumptions and potential weaknesses to the system, they continue instead to slave away, work fifty weeks of the year and hope that someday they will rise from the server at McDonald's, either make manager and own one of those, or come up with a brilliant idea in the hours off work and be as rich and famous as Mark. Yeah, that guy of Facebook.

The American capitalist economic system is quite fundamentally flawed. First, it assumes that there is an infinite supply of resources – natural and human. The system also assumes that individuals can rise to some undetermined level of success. This is not the case.

There are finite resources, and their more equitable distribution would be a more balanced approach to having an equitable society. However, this is probably not a good point to raise, because one will be accused of being socialist / communist. Societies that divide their resources in more equitable ways are far much happier; then again, who said life was about happiness?

Secondly, the people who work hardest are often rewarded least. The team of cashiers, loaders, and cleaners at Wal-Mart most likely works harder than anyone of the members of the Walton family. On the other hand, the argument might be made that since their father came up with the idea of Wal-Mart, the heirs should enjoy the fruits of their hard work and their father's imagination.

Right there is the major fallacy in the whole economic model. As a company, Wal-Mart is valued at about 24 billion dollars, but because of the wages that are paid to the millions of minions who work for the bosses, Americans have to heavily subsidize the lifestyles of these workers: studies have shown a very high number of these workers on Food Stamps and on Medicaid. It is well known that these programs were established to support the poor and low-income persons in American society.

So, in essence, American daily shoppers subsidize the major companies' employees (these include Starbucks, Belk and others), so that their bosses, using the profits reaped from the same American daily shoppers, can accrue their values to several billion. It is these same bosses and owners of industry who turn around and accuse 47 percent of America of being moochers as they seek votes to elect them into office.

Thirdly, the system assumes that everyone starts from the same place, and that they can then progress forward. It glosses over the historical facts of the difficulty in everyone getting ahead, and continues to propagate a myth that everyone in America can make it, if they try hard enough. This is not true. Some people accrued their resources a long time ago, when resources included people, or when some people provided free labor especially for the *bourgeoisie* class.

Fourth, the value of the economic system, the products and services is grossly overvalued. Wall Street is a prime example, as is the real estate market. It is all based on *perception*. Here is how you know this: property values begin to plummet if there are several crimes committed within a neighborhood, or if drug activity begins to happen if a railway line is built or if public buses begin to traverse a neighborhood.

Nothing about the houses or street changes; that is, except the perception that the neighborhood is probably unsafe. Similarly, with Wall Street, Apple Stock might plummet one day based on unspecified market perception; the value, components and sale price of Apple products does not have to change for the perception to change and for the stock to plummet or rise.

The economic system therefore assumes the character of a house of cards: it can collapse at any time, without cause or reason. It is a system that is based on perception, rather than on manufacturing.

Permanent Workers

The economic system – buttressed by the education and other social systems – are a lifetime, unending conveyor belt – of "worker production". American society teaches its members the value of hard work, daily work, work during vacation, but rarely teaches its members how to innovate, become entrepreneurs – which makes sense; you can't have too many entrepreneurs. The system has learnt from the ant kingdom: division of labor, with most of the work being performed by labourers, who are also, by default, the majority.

The system has invented checks and balances, perks and punishments. Everything becomes connected; from internships that turn into jobs, longevity in employment, qualification for loans and housing based on employment history; in other words, the economic system ties everything together and ensures that workers will be reliable or they will lose their 401K's, their houses, their credit rating and all other vignettes of modern day economic slavery (or if you like, progress).

Americans deride the French – and most every other

nation – for everything from cheese to work habits. Yet, they spend every 50 weeks out of 52 weeks working their lives off, on average working 40 hours a week and getting 30 minutes of lunch break on average, working several jobs to make ends meet, and believing this is normal. Well, one argument that can be made for this is that Americans are hard-working. It is not evident that their hard work pays, or that all the work produces any particularly favourable outcome with regard to giving them a better quality of life.

Health Insurance

The American economic system long ago figured out how to blackmail its workers to stay on the job: make health insurance one of the most desirable benefits (perhaps with complicity from the food industry which generally does not share the view of providing health insurance for its workers), and tie it to employment. First off, it is ridiculous that an individual's life depends on insurance, but that is a wholly different argument. Linking health insurance to employment is genius; it provides two incentives at the price of one.

Of course, the idea of changing the form and provision of health insurance has been one of the most contentious aspects of American society (in fairness, any idea that resembles another idea from another country or resembles change quite often finds very little traction. It is an admirable quality, but then, the dinosaurs became extinct because they could not adapt.

Retirement

From the first day on the job, every American is practically inculcated with the idea that retirement is the ultimate objective (that, and owning a home). Some of the key variables in the selection of a job, where an individual has options, is the possibility of having benefits, including that 401K with matching by the employer.

It is amazing how much America plans for retirement – even when you just started working at 18. It is somewhat depressing to be thinking about retirement when most Americans – at least 85 percent of them – generally never travel more than 15 miles from home; it gives one the concept of a goat, tethered to the same spot, immobile.

It is further depressing that most Americans retire in some kind of old folks' home – you know, as opposed to retiring in Belize, what with the good weather, decent hospitals, low cost of living and proximity to the United States – and they also do speak American.

Education and economic success

Education is one of the major determinants of, and avenues for upward social and economic mobility for the American society. Well-educated individuals can generally expect to have better lives; however, education also produces great inequality. This is especially the case given the level of education and the college one chooses to attend. Contrary to what most people believe, education is one of the greatest contributors to inequality.

What most Americans fail to grasp is that the world runs on the "old boy system"; if you attend an Ivy League school this almost instantly opens you up to opportunities someone going to a third-rate community college in Wyoming can only dream of. Of course, there are opportunities for economic and social mobility, and education provides some of those, and the old boy network takes care of the rest – including ensuring that they get all the best jobs and in the same industry.

Taxes and educational funding

One of the most intriguing, not in a nice way, aspects of American public policy is the method by which education is funded. Most school districts use the property tax (base) to fund schools. By definition, this is perhaps the most unequal method of funding schools anyone could possibly come up with.

Consider this: if a school, or couple of schools, are in an area where the property values are quite low (Detroit, for instance). Next, because the school funding budget is based on property taxes, and they happen to be low because the taxes are low since the property taxes are low, it is not possible to generate a lot of money to fund schools.

Now, remember the myth about how everyone can pull themselves up by their bootstraps and that everyone can achieve if they really try? That is halfway true; not everyone has the same kinds of resources, so they do not go to all kinds of programs like Lacrosse, piano lessons, after school programs and what have you.

Schools in the low income areas are resource-deficient and their students do not have the same opportunities as students from higher tax-base schools. As a result, they are exposed to fewer programs and extra-curricular activities and their resumes look thinner. They have less exposure to the kind of programs that would drive them to succeed and offer them opportunities to go to those Ivy League schools.

It is amazing that despite the rhetoric of *"all men are created equal and are endowed by their creator with certain inalienable rights"*, the probability of all kids in the United States having the same outcome in life is generally not true. One's station in life is by and large determined by five digits – the Zip Code. If one child's parents are disadvantaged enough to live in a low income area, it is improbable that their child will generally have a different outcome in life.

It would make much more sense if educational funding was done through a national educational fund. That way, despite the background that each individual child comes from, they would have a fair shot at the proverbial American Dream. Naturally, that might not be desirable to a host of folks. Of course, the reality is wholly different:

some schools get metal detectors, while others get Lacrosse lessons.

The priorities – economic and social – of any great country should contribute to some form of equality among all persons. It is not evident that the American system has made this even plausible.

China's debt

One of the constraints to the greatest nation's economy is the size of its debt. Granted, this has never stopped the government from doing what it needs to do – give its citizens raises and spend obscene amounts of money in Iraq and Afghanistan or continue borrowing. Between them, China and Japan own a very sizeable tranche of the US economy, and it ought to bother someone – mostly Americans – that their government is borrowing so much from the orient to pay for stuff.

The culture of saving is quite alien to most of the United States. There is almost this perception that there is no end to the source of money. Americans have this notion that by spending on stuff, somehow their lives improves. And since the Chinese have learnt that they can make crappy stuff and sell it to the Americans with money that they lend to the Americans – obviously at some handsome interest margin – it is a win-win for the Chinese, especially, since said Americans will then spend their fleeting lives borrowing money from the Chinese to buy Chinese products that make them more miserable – especially when they are laced with lead.

There is an aspect of just disliking the Chinese and highlighting their debt, mainly because the Chinese are considered communist. In truth, the Japanese own almost an equally substantial part of the US debt at about 6% (compared to China at 8%), the UK at 2.5% (so UK and Japan own about the same portion of the debt as China). Other countries are owed twice as much as China, while the Social Security Fund and others are owed about 17%;

the US government owes the public close to 40%.

Very few governments and countries are debt free; it is something inherent in the DNA of governments. Now, the US Republican party would like perhaps to see Southern California hived off and sold to the Chinese to pay off the Chinese and Japanese and also get rid of the "moral issue", but then they remember that they probably have a few friends during campaigns and might need some money so they will keep California.

It is not impossible to pay the debt the US owes, but it is not clear that it is desirable (only when Andrew Jackson was president was the US debt-free – so let's resurrect him...on the other hand, let's not: crappy person – and all American Indians say Amen). Perhaps managing it more, fighting fewer wars, giving fewer breaks to the oligarchs and the Koch billionaires and the Rockefellers might save the country some money. In addition to a national campaign to quit buying useless, lead-laced Chinese crap.

A perception economy

At a conference a few years ago, a Russian scholar made the point that an economy based on nothing but perception: manufacturing had moved from Detroit and other small-towns America and was now concentrated in – here we go again, Shanghai, China! He argued that a nation stops being great when it stops manufacturing things and begins buying everything from others. For

Considering he was Russian, he was probably biased, but it made perfect sense; an economy needs to create stuff, to manufacture things that can be sold. This means that the particular economy has raw materials, labor and some capital and also the technology. Think of the modern US economy: several times in the recent past it has been shaken by events happening as far as Thailand and Japan and so on (and I don't mean earthquakes and landslides). The proposition here is that it is a bubble economy, which manufactures just about nothing but hope.

The 2007-8 stock market crash (or, as politely known, the Great Recession), caused allegedly by a housing bubble (people bought stuff they could not afford, in this case, homes) illustrated just how much bubble there was. The value of something manufactured depreciates at a specific amount over a specific time; that is not the case with the bubble economy. For instance, a Chrysler imported from Detroit might depreciate depending on how its driven (mileage) over a number of days (time).

The bubble economy, when it bursts, loses billions of dollars over a very short period of time. Of course, it makes sense! There is nothing that Apple, for instance, makes, that is worth $500 (except perhaps an iPhone) per share. It is the perception, the expectation (and some might say, the greed) that Apple might invent something earth-shattering. It is hype, driven by other hyped up people; it is the perception of the value of knowledge and potential (it is still not clear why a company stock would plummet that quickly unless we lose faith in the potential).

Take a home, for example. In theory, it should be worth as much as the materials that were used to construct it, plus the value of the land that it is built on. Now, because we live in a perception / bubble economy, the value of the house or property inflates based on the perception of self and others about factors such as the probability that one will be shot while getting shot, or the pass rate at the local high school, or the number of wins its high school has.

While no economist, it seems that the Russian was right, and the American's propensity to purchase stuff that they generally cannot afford, or focus on inflating the value and meaning of things, does not bode well for the future of its economy.

The good thing is that Wal-Mart, which facilitated shipping all manufacturing jobs abroad (for the most part – Chrysler helped, by going broke, and being bought by Fiat, which now manufactures those ugly Fiats in Mexico) – is returning jobs to these United States. One hopes that the lesson for actually building and making stuff – much as Henry Ford and World War II did – will be learned.

Consumerism

The practice of consumerism is very widespread, almost a way of life. Take for instance celebrations. In these United States it is almost impossible to have a celebration – birthday, Christmas (renamed happy holidays), Thanksgiving, Easer (spring break) and everything in between – especially birthdays – without accruing a lot of worthless crap from the Chinese. There is a perception that celebrations must be accompanied by endless streams of prizes, cards, flowers and stuff no one needs. The more stuff one gets, the bigger the perception that one is loved.

For many years I have even puzzled whether kids who are growing up in this age, in this formerly Christian nation, even know the origin or meaning of the "happy holidays", formerly (and everywhere else) known as Christmas holidays. For them, it is about some oversized white dude (yes, he is white, remember that teacher who categorically stated that Santa was white?) coming down the chimney (woe if you don't have a chimney in your rented apartment) and presents under a Christmas tree (some of them fake, again, sold by the Chinese).

Consumerism is evident, and often at its best, during the holidays. This criticism does not imply that people do not need stuff; it is the sheer scale and dedication that is nothing short of amazing. Many years ago, Thanksgiving (paradoxically, Thanksgiving for arriving in the New World and subsequently mass-murdering Native Americans and taking most of their land) used to be an occasion for merry, family and such. Then, Black Friday came about (why did they have to pick on the ex-slaves – black?) and it became food, family, fun and then shopping. It marked the beginning of the crazy frenzy that would last the whole season through "happy holidays" until January.

Now, since stores are fretting that their customers are

not buying enough (really?), they have taken to beginning the shopping season even earlier: some stores have violated the sanctity of Thanksgiving and now it starts on the very day. It is in doubt which of the two will win: turkey or shopping; my bet is on the latter.

Oh, yes, we forgot to mention: the money that folks are using to shop is generally borrowed – some from the Chinese. This is the recipe for the fall of a great nation: through sheer greed and not appreciating that stuff does not make one happy; indeed, they would be much happier spending more time with family than lining up for several hours to several days to get the newest iPad, iPod and the rest of the Black Friday and the rest of the shopping season.

Chapter 6
The Social welfare system

The Social Welfare system in the United States is one of the most innovative inventions of the government. Of course, it can be explained away in several ways: it was designed to be some half-hearted atonement for the treatment of the black folks after slavery given that they suddenly became citizens with the average education and possibility of survival of a Somali national. Or it could have been genuine compassion for folks who did not have enough to eat and heat their houses. Or, it could have been a control mechanism by the federal government to suppress potential insurrection.

When people are hungry, poor, frustrated and have not enough to eat, it is useful for a government to consider that this is a recipe for social unrest. Social unrest has caused governments to be overthrown. Hungry people have nothing to lose, and as a result, everything becomes legitimate. Including violence. So, the clever thing to do is to ensure that folks have enough to eat, and as a result, are less likely to do anything that imperils government.

Of course, there are valid reasons for having a robust social welfare system. The United States goes through several weather changes, and the only time when people are unlikely to freeze to death or to die of heat exhaustion are the spring and fall. The winter and the summer require some way of mitigating the climate. Additionally, most folks have no land or have ceased to become farmers (mainly, because they have been thrown out of the business of farming by big corporations).

The social welfare system allows the beneficiaries to mooch on the government (at least some people do), while for some it provides a needed safety net until they find the next job or the next lottery win. The moochers, unfortunately, have found ways of not working, relying on the system through generations. If only the government could send them to Somalia they might figure out that they can actually work and not die and provide for themselves.

As a safety net, it works well (and costs so little that the folks at the bottom do not have cause to ask questions), and keeps the beneficiaries so dependent that they are unlikely to upset the system for fear of losing these "benefits". What the beneficiaries have generally failed to conceive is that for example, TANF (Temporary Assistance for Needy Families) may pay $236 a month.

Over 12 months, this comes to about $3000, give or take some. Add Food Stamps (SNAP, they are called these days) at, say, $600 for a family of 5, that comes to about $7200. Add Medicaid, say $100 per person per month, and you have another about $7200, give or take. So, a family of 5 may subsist on $20,000 (and may get rental assistance in form of subsidized housing, paying, say, $60 a month rather than $1200 for a 4-br house. So, really, the math adds up and the $14000 and $20000 adds up to approximately $35000.

If one were to milk that much from the government for a year, it is understandable why getting a job that makes $30,000 may not make much sense. The creation of a dependency culture facilitates the recipients to do nothing but collect checks, exchange food stamps for cigarettes and spend all day being reproductive. Plus, there is always the trick of working a few months in the year in order to qualify for the Child Tax Credit. It is a perfect system, and works for everyone.

Except, the social welfare system is much akin to the mental health system. The mental health system works like this: an individual is diagnosed with a major diagnosis.

They are declared "disabled" and get a monthly check for about $700, give or take some change. They have to take numerous psychotropic medications, which are paid for by Medicaid, which is paid for by the American public through taxes.

So, the beneficiaries of the Medicaid system have psychiatrists, therapists and case managers and a whole treatment team, and they get paid off the same Medicaid, in what is called the Supplemental Security Income. It sort of works like the social welfare system: the idea is to ensure that the "disabled" persons do not experience serious hardships. Of course the greatest beneficiary is the pharmaceutical companies. But everyone down the particular food chain benefits.

So does the social welfare system. Four kids are a handful to take care of; they require all kinds of resources, attention, play dates, proms and such. They get sick, they have homework...it becomes quite a task to bring them up. With poor parenting skills, most parents are driven to drugs, drink or just not to care. So the kids enter a cycle of low achievement, and repeat the cycle over and over in the not too far future.

Of course, some of the parents are generally too happy collecting the welfare check, hoarding food (noodles is a favourite), and smoking cigarettes and doing other drugs. Quite a high percentage of the parents who find themselves in this cycle also have very low levels of education, which makes it extremely difficult to exit from such a system.

The incentives are not there either: why work if you can collect several thousand dollars in food stamps, TANF and other kinds of monies (for example, if your kids are diagnosed with mental health illnesses and disabilities) from the state. Understandably, there are constant efforts to reform the system every few years, and every so often some politician puts his foot in the mouth and calls it like he sees it (remember Romney's 47% comment?)

It is, of course, easy to criticize superficially, without knowing or understanding the full value of ensuring that a country is doing the best with the resources that they have to take care of their populations. After all, it is generally agreed that the true measure of a nation is obtained by how a society treats the weakest members of its society. It would be unconscionable to leave children and women in the streets to die of heat exhaustion or freeze to death, or starve to death. It makes perfect sense to provide all possible resources to take care of its people, especially the weakest.

The tragedy of the social welfare system, especially the SNAP part and the TANF parts, is not the amount of money it consumes. It is much more in the talent it wastes, by allowing some of the professional welfare recipients to continue to draw benefits by any means possible. If there was a threat of starving to death, it is not clear that they would not do things differently.

The bigger issue is one of how much even the recipients lose. While the $30,000 that a five-family member accrues over one year from benefits (some of it may not be fully used, for instance the medical part) sounds like a pile of money, it is important to consider what they are NOT getting. The $30,000 is about the average cost for attending one year of a 4-year college degree.

Of course it is not in the interest of a country to have everyone equally educated, since then they might get to be so smart that the government no longer has a good hold on them and possibly impede their freedoms as easily.

The recipients, however, do not calculate it that way. Divided among the five family members, this is only $6000 or thereabouts per person per year. Conversely, FAFSA may provide the same amount of money, to pay for college, and exponentially increase the earning potential of an individual once they graduate college. Of course, instant gratification is part of the genetic makeup for some people, so it is not very helpful to be thinking about the long-term.

An estimated $2.5 billion is available for individuals who are willing to go to school - in form of scholarships and fellowships in the United States alone. Even without borrowing money from government or other lenders, it is so possible to go to school and graduate and improve one's life. Again, it may be a question of laziness. Why do anything, if you can just sit and get a check and really not do much in way of putting an effort towards accomplishing anything?

The other problem with the social welfare system is that even those who advocate for its modification, change or eventual elimination fail to confront the real issues: the so called moochers are not willing to really change their approach to life. What if the recipients were required to, as a condition for eligibility, to complete two years of school?

There should be a requirement that if they had no GED, for the first time they apply for eligibility, they should be required to obtain one. The next time they apply, they would be required to obtain an associate's degree. Somewhere within this whole philosophy, the beneficiaries would also interact with different ideas and perhaps begin to be contributors to the economy and see the potential for their earning if they applied themselves and changed the moocher mentality.

Now, there is nothing to say that obtaining an associate's degree or any other academic qualification will necessarily change their approach to wanting free things. The idea of exposing such persons to other ways of thinking, showing them what might be possible if they had a different lifestyle, giving them other sources of information – would perhaps change the way that they approach the idea of their role as citizens in a democracy, and make them more productive rather than reproductive.

In a democracy, the ability to choose is one of the most important values. What democracies have not decided to engage with in a reasonably robust way is whether this freedom to make choices should imply that other people in the same democracy should have to support the particular individual's choices.

If, for instance, an individual decides to have three or four children whom they cannot support - or are not willing to support - what should others in the democracy do? Clearly, anyone making babies without a way to support them should either be sent to a labor camp or neutered. But that, in a democracy, should be a very contentious topic. That is why sometimes autocracies work better - look at how successful China's one-child policy has been.

A useful system

There are non-system systems that have produced very different results. Somalia, for example, stands in contrast and as an example of the countries that do not have any social welfare systems or means to take care of its weakest and most vulnerable. It was, of course, the scene of the "great rescue" that ended up as the "great debacle" in 1992. If they had had a social welfare system, many things would not have happened: the US would not have lost face and a bunch of people would not have starved. Neither would those millions in Ethiopia in the 1980s.

Most other developing countries do not have systems designed to protect the most vulnerable. Instead, they just allow their citizens to either starve, scrounge around for food and other resources to meet their needs. Of course, there is no better motivator than having no form of support: it makes people more resourceful and hard working.

It also has the potential to make them more violent: hunger causes all kinds of resources. It potentially leads to more probability for riots and violent government changes. This sometimes does backfire and leads to people becoming pirates. Perhaps the US should send out some of its welfare recipients to the countries that do not have any social welfare systems and teach them about the value of hard work.

The closing thought on the US social welfare system is this: there are good, solid benefits to having a robust system that ensures that children of irresponsible and down-on-their-luck parents do not starve. It is also good to design a system that ensures that people do not become dependent, and that the system is a backup, not a way of life. The system should be designed to ensure that everyone benefitting from it understands this.

More importantly, it is important to retain the system given that the climatic conditions in the US do not lend themselves to leaving people to fend for themselves. And after all, the true measure of a people is how they treat their weakest members of society. Just don't let them become too dependent or the country will spend most of its resources supporting non-productive people.

Chapter 7
Religion and Morality

Religion in the United States remains quite a controversial subject. The primary lines of division are reflected in the US Constitution, in the First Amendment regarding the establishment of religion versus freedom of worship. On the one hand, no one can be prevented from worshipping the god of their choice, even if that is a tree god, as long as in theory, the worship does not violate the basic human rights or US law. This is not necessarily strictly adhered to: think of bigamy and the Mormon Church and therein begin the contradictions.

The United States produced some of the earliest instances of missionaries; folks who moved out of the King's Realm of oppression and not only found freedom, but also brought Christianity to the New World. As such, the United States' founding fathers (yes, there were just fathers, the women were - shall we say - in the kitchen) leaned towards the United States being a predominantly Christian nation. Not only was it predominantly Christian; it was specifically a WASP nation (White Anglo Saxon Protestant) nation.

Today, religion is not just about Jesus Christ - and other lesser or greater gods. It is about whether religion commands an inordinate amount of attention, more than it perhaps should. It is about the freedom NOT to worship, about taking off the motto from the dollar bill, about making the US a secular nation. Of course nations evolve, change, and grow (or grown backwards).

Materialism has also been on the rise, and has quite eroded the need for God. As people discovered technology, medicine and other things that allow them to control their environment, their faith began to erode and the instances in which they would have called on God began to reduce. Of course, if one watches the opening of any NASCAR race, one will be reminded of the importance of God. But then, maybe that is just a southern, redneck thing: that section of society that seems to be planted sometime between the 1920's and the 1950's. It is possible to achieve economic development and progress and still have faith.

Religion in the United States is on the decline, and is under attack from practically every front; the only place where religion appears to have a few remaining friends is the courts - especially in the South. Secular groups, including equal-rights groups, appear to be winning the battle against the traditional Christian lifestyle and religious beliefs. The very core of the Christian beliefs has been challenged, with gay and lesbian Bishops being anointed, in the belief that Sodom and Gomorrah were historical anomalies and that God should not care who anyone sleeps with.

This has led to a situation where Christians are literally barricaded; in Church, and in their communities. They have started radio stations, broadcasting to each other and the small segment they can still win from the devil. They have formed Conferences and Colleges, and are increasingly seeing their Christian base eroded. They are, however, fighting back, and at the highest levels, with regard to the Presidency, they could be winning some.

Studying the decline of the Great Christian nation is quite interesting. It has shown that as a country progresses, they may gain on the one hand but lose on the other. The paradox is that religion does not have to be oppositional to progress. They can co-exist. The human being without faith in something other than themselves is akin to an empty shell. There are lots of empty shells walking around in this neighborhood. But then, this is the measure of progress.

Muslims and others

Religious tolerance is important; it is practically, after tolerance within ethnic divisions, the one way in which we can gauge the level of civilization of a people. The United States cannot be said to be a religiously tolerant nation; in fact, it is only tolerant when the religion is Christianity.

The United States was founded as a Christian nation. This is so reflected for example in its motto, "In God We Trust." Perhaps it should have been clarified that it was the Christian God that was trusted, not any other. And while the Constitution guarantees freedom of worship, it is not evident that some - like the Sikhs found - can worship freely, mainly due to the ignorance of some sections of the American society. It is okay to practice religion; just practice the 'right' religion.

Presidential politics are a time of reflection about religious pluralism and religious intolerance. They are also an opportunity for the United States and the rest of the world to discover just how much religiously intolerant the United States is. Take for example Camelot - the first and only Catholic President in US presidential history. During his campaigns, he had to go on national TV and reassure the American public that he was not going to be taking orders from the Pope if he was elected President. Of course, a president's moral and religious compass is important, but for St. Pete's sake, taking orders from the Pope? Really?

The drama was repeated close to four decades later, when one Willard Mitt Romney ran for president. You see, Willard is the gentleman who co-founded Bain Capital, a very successful investment firm. His great sins included calling half of the American population "moochers". His really greatest sin, the one that could have sent him to hell, was that he was a Mormon, and there were murmurs of concern that he might require every American to begin engaging in polygamy or worship some dubious god. It point sto a general lack of information on the part of the public; it is not very clear that Willard would have been taking his orders from the Mormon Bishop; rather, he was more likely to take his orders from Wall Street. After all, it is a money society.

Gay and Lesbian persons

Is a gay lifestyle a lifestyle, a choice or a genetic predisposition? One might ask the same of the predisposition for some men to take two wives, or to cheat on their partners (or even vice versa). Of course, there are studies showing that some people are attracted to people of their own gender, the opposite gender or both genders. That is quite interesting, especially given the changes over time in who could sleep with who and also given the two sides' beliefs about homosexuality being a choice versus a genetic predisposition.

On a personal level, it is unimportant to me who sleeps with who. What is interesting is the minority-majority status, the perception that being gay is a genetic predisposition, and those individuals who are not recognized and their unions respected are being discriminated against. The concept and acceptability of gay/lesbian relationships in the United States has accelerated, with such relationships now legal in quite a number of states, and being seen as the next big thing after the civil rights.

Societies can collectively decide what direction they want to take, morally, spiritually and even sexually. It is one thing to accept within one's nation that such relationships are okay, it is another to force others to accept the same. After all, isn't the United States unique in many ways? Maybe it is the only place where there are gay persons. A private opinion to be expressed only in this particular forum is that while it is not my business who sleeps with who, if enough people have relationships with members of their same gender, the birth-rate might approximate that of Italy – and the Italians are not even that gay. It is not clear to me that I would be in such a relationship - but, if the American society has decided on its demise based on inability to reproduce, then so be it. Of course, the probability of getting pregnant reduces to almost zero, so that is a positive.

Morality and choices

A society that does not have a moral, or has a shifting moral compass, is one destined to go the way of the dinosaur. There has to be a collective set of beliefs that are the foundation of a society, otherwise a society with no foundation basically has no chance of long-term survival. The issue of gay and lesbian acceptance, as well as how countries deal with it, is especially important to review. It is very unfortunate that free countries are compelled to decide what is morally acceptable for them and their citizens.

It is amazing how much the US pushes other countries to adopt their moral choices regarding their perception and treatment of gay/lesbian persons. It is very difficult, and perhaps unwarranted, to try and make others accept your moral choices, without compelling evidence that what you propose is actually supported by irrefutable fact.

Here is the paradox: when Uganda - and many other African countries decided that it was against their cultures to allow gay/lesbian persons the same rights as the rest of their citizens, the US led an international campaign to restrict and rescind foreign aid

First and foremost, the average Ugandan is probably not worried about who is sleeping with whom, and even if a guy/guy or girl/girl relationship happens, it still won't give them food to eat. So, to deny folks aid that could mean their very existence just because they object to the moral choice other people have made sounds like a very unfortunate and unfair course of action.

Isn't it ironic that the very Christians who introduced the religion to the very countries they now have an active campaign against, have now changed course and decided that the reasons why Sodom and Gomorrah were torched by the Almighty can now be ignored, and we can all sleep with everyone - men, women and such?

Here is a counterpoint: why would the US accept that gay and lesbian relationships are okay, but that polygamy is not? What if that is how some people were born? What is the compelling reason to deny a polygamous marriage? Economically - as we have seen with the Saudis - it is possible to support more than one wife.

So, why is it illegal/against the law to marry more than one person? No one has advanced compelling reasons. After all, it was quite acceptable in 1957 to bar blacks from marrying whites and vice versa; and then that changed. It was also not acceptable to have gay/lesbian relationships; so perhaps we shall evolve and Mormonism will be quite acceptable.

Morality in the United States appears to be relative. Two hundred years ago; nay, one hundred and sixty years ago, it was morally acceptable to have slaves. Then suddenly it was not. Until sixty years ago, it was morally right to consider blacks second-class citizens, unequal. Suddenly morality shifted and the United States discovered that "all men (and women) are created equal."

It is a very interesting case of relativity in morality. One wonders, after the gay/lesbian issue, what else will become morally relative.

Marriage

Once upon a time, kids, there was a man and a woman. They liked each other a lot, and could not stand being apart from each other. The man asked the woman if she could come stay with him, and together they would be happy and start a family and all that. The woman agreed and they moved in together; before they did, however, they went to the Judge/Priest and he joined them together in marriage. And that, folks, was how marriage came about into being.

Okay, maybe that is not how it came into being. But for the longest time in history, marriage was defined (at least in the United States) as a union between a man and a woman. In other places, it was often defined as a union between one man and many women, one woman and many men, or many men and many women (it is not clear what that would have been).

Then, life happened and a man and another man thought they could live together, and soon found out that their friends were doing the same thing, and that there were two women doing the same thing...and soon, a movement to change the definition of marriage from a union between a man and a woman started; the ideal definition was going to be a union between any two consenting adults, never mind their gender.

The rest of the world, of course, was collectively shocked and did not want this new moral standard imposed on them. So some countries moved to outlaw the notion that marriage could mean anything other than a union between a man and a woman or a man and several women. The concept of same sex relationship was revolting to them and they balked.

Remember the whole Christianity thing? Apparently those countries held onto the teachings that the very Americans who had begun the process of formalization of marriage were now changing. FYI, Americans: there is an unhealthy obsession with pieces of paper - which have replaced community. My parents have been married about 52 years now, and there is not a piece of paper that was signed to legitimate their marriage; but everyone knows they are married. True, for the sake of "benefits" it may be necessary to have paperwork, but the world is different!

Redefining marriage is not a good thing. It will open all doors to all kinds of people with all kinds of money, who can change the perception of what our reality is. If some guy decided that marrying a 15 year old is genetically predisposed, how are we going to top them? How can we justify that it is not? There was a girl called Pandora, and she had a box...

Race

There is nothing as important in these United States as the concept of race. True, no one talks about it openly, but it is practically the first thing that anyone notices. It is further affirmed in documentation: most forms that Americans fill are accompanied by the choice of race categories. It would be easier to just have two categories: us and them; white and others.

There is a hypothesized equality between all races in the said United States, but that is true only on paper. There is a hierarchy of race, and it is so well hidden that even the federal forms and anti-discriminatory practices cannot change that fact. Race has been an integral part of the United States and its society and generally defines everything that happens in the country. It is a hidden determinant for wealth, prosperity, where people live, what college one goes to and all that.

Of course, all races have not been treated equally. In fact, the founding fathers of these United States did not consider anyone other than White Men "people". The beauty of the Preamble to the US Constitution makes this clear, especially when it speaks of "All Men are Created Equal." Of course slaves were not men; they were not equal to humans.

The issue of race persists in the United States; it is its worst Achilles Heel. The Civil Rights Act and all that means nothing if you can still be discriminated on a job application just because you are black or have a "different" name. It is especially interesting to see how the US requires equal treatment of minorities while race continues to be one of its weaknesses.

Chapter 8
Closing thoughts: We The Sissy People

It is no secret that the United States has some capabilities going for it, but there are many ways to conceive of a great nation. A foreigner living in the United States might appreciate the benefits of living in these United States, but there are also very many negatives to living here.

For starters, the 30,000 gun deaths give anyone from, say, Botswana where police officers carry batons, pause. Some parts of the United States feel more dangerous than Baghdad or Beirut. Think, for example, of Compton, Detroit and Newport News. You could get shot while getting shot.

Living in these United States could also shorten your life considerably. The combination of the stress, the bad food - mostly, GMO foods - and other lifestyle changes, including the very fast pace that life takes, requires that after 60, which is towards the end of the life, that one be on rather numerous medications.

The whole irony in this is that most Americans spend most of their working lives saving money for retirement, except no one tells them that they will be on so much medication it will be difficult to tell east from west, or that after you retire, you have no energy to do anything at all!

The death of community is one of the most negative aspects of the United States. It is such an individualistic society and everyone cares for just themselves. Everyone else's business becomes just that: it is only when there is a national calamity that people do what people do in other places: be kind to their neighbors. There is need to rethink the whole community idea; it takes too much effort to be around other human beings. Human beings were made to be social.

Americans are generally ignorant of the rest of the world. There is a self-absorption about them that is amazingly naive. Even when they fight wars, they have no conception of where those places they fight are - unless, of course, they are stationed there. They generally do not know their geography, politics or anything else of importance other than their lives, their pets, baseball, stores, gym, football, NASCAR and other mundane things in their lives.

They show a very low level of interest even in the politics of their own backyards, and have little conception of especially other peoples' histories. Granted, it is not clear that the Russians know much about the history of Tuvalu or of Malawi, but they do not purport – except on Tuesdays and Thursdays – pretend to run the world. If you run the world, it is good to know something about the world you run. Or the cavemen and insurgents will teach you lessons of geopolitics and political history. It is also useful to learn that there is no country called Africa and to really conceive that other countries out there also believe – with all their hearts – that they are equally great.

There is a compartmentalization, a sense of good and bad/evil that overlooks the shades of grey. With due apologies to those Americans who see the shades of grey and colour scales, it is good to not look at the world in terms of black or white. The world is an exceedingly complex place, and even things that we do not think affect us, sometimes have the capacity to do so.

The world is inhabited by more than Americans; so for instance, if there is a climate change debate, it is not just about you and your truck – or your Prius – it is much more than that. Also, realize that the poor Syrian may actually have to burn some wood, not because they want to pollute, but because they want to be warm and cook and have no access to electricity.

Americans are a complacent people. Especially when it comes to the notion of security, they are very unquestioning about their elected officials even when the premise is basically fallacious. Take the extreme security regimen that now punctuates air travel, especially within the United States. Why would it be unconscionable to "screen" every "terrorist-looking" individual and screen them, instead of screening and molesting grandmothers and 9 year olds?

Really, they are going to be blowing up airliners? Why does one go through more rigorous screening going to a Social Security office than going through the airport? Most attacks come from outside (except the one, you know), but Americans have willingly given in to the police state and now are routinely molested in the name of security.

There is an inexplicable attention and obsession to "protecting." There is an almost "siege mentality" among Americans, that they need to be "protected" from practically everything. Whether it is a fire (the victims need to be protected) or an accident - there is either an overuse of the concept of protection, or Americans genuinely feel threatened by some element out there. It is not clear when this began to happen, but it is understandable that if one perhaps goes around bombing different places and watches too much CNN, then they might get the siege mentality.

The attitude towards guns is also quite interesting. It is not clear why anyone would want to eat a cheeseburger with a gun in their holster; it either bespeaks a people, a country that is so insecure that one expects to fully lose their cheeseburger to a horde of invading hungry aliens - or citizens - or that they have so many enemies that it is necessary to protect themselves. After all, isn't this the best, most powerful, most secure country in the world? It is not certain that even in Kabul, Beirut, Port-au-Prince or

Baghdad, the militias eat shish-kebabs with their hands on their AK-47's.

Of course the issue of guns arouses quite the sentiment among the people. The rather sad discussion goes like this: the Second Amendment to the US constitution allows individuals the right to carry guns. Ok, so maybe one doesn't trust their fellow citizens to the extent that they feel they need to shoot them every so often. The more nuanced argument is that the right to carry guns is in the event that the government turns Saddam-Iraq-like, and the citizens need a way to fight the government.

What is amusing about this particular argument is that it is not clear whether an M-4, which appears to be the most lethal gun class that a regular citizen can own, is capable of shooting down a Minuteman III missile, or a nuclear bomb, if indeed there was a crazy enough general to launch one in the name of the government on the people. If the government decides to turn on the people – remember Waco, Texas? Not all the 300 million guns in these United States will make a difference.

The most that the guns do is facilitate 30,000 deaths a year, mostly because Americans have lost the ability to settle arguments like everyone else: with a good-old fist. Every argument quickly degenerates into a gunfight. This is what makes the United States such a dangerous place. It would be quite something for Americans to begin thinking about re-learning to fight with fists rather than with guns.

Threats from outside the country have made the country more prone to erosions in a variety of issues and fronts. Democracy and freedom, in these United States, have been gradually eroded by the money and peddling influence, the police-state mentality arising from insecurity, and these threaten to erode the quality of life in these United States. The Government, with capital G, has taken upon itself to spy on its citizens, further degrading the quality of life.

One might want to pick up a map – remember "The

Next Three Days" and look towards, say, Belize. The government of Belize has not quite mastered how to spy on its citizens, the climate is good, one can always travel - including to Cuba - for medical treatment and also enjoy a higher quality of life.

To use a well-worn statement, "all that glitters is not gold." The greatest nation on earth is too hyped. There are other great nations out there. Such as Finland or Sweden. Or Botswana. The greatest nation on earth does have flaws, and any great nation takes stock of these weaknesses and improves constantly.

The End